PRIVACY IN
THE DIGITAL AGE

CELL PHONE
PRIVACY

BY HEATHER C. HUDAK

CONTENT CONSULTANT
M. E. Kabay, PhD, CISSP-ISSMP
Professor of Computer Information Systems
Norwich University

Core Library

Cover image: Cell phones with facial recognition
software unlock when they recognize a user's face.

An Imprint of Abdo Publishing
abdobooks.com

abdocorelibrary.com

Published by Abdo Publishing, a division of ABDO, PO Box 398166,
Minneapolis, Minnesota 55439. Copyright © 2020 by Abdo Consulting
Group, Inc. International copyrights reserved in all countries. No part of this
book may be reproduced in any form without written permission from the
publisher. Core Library™ is a trademark and logo of Abdo Publishing.

Printed in the United States of America, North Mankato, Minnesota
042019
092019

THIS BOOK CONTAINS
RECYCLED MATERIALS

Cover Photo: Artem Oleshko/Shutterstock Images
Interior Photos: Artem Oleshko/Shutterstock Images, 1; People Images/iStockphoto, 4–5;
Red Line Editorial, 7, 12; Shutterstock Images, 10–11, 18–19, 43; Susan Law Cain/Shutterstock
Images, 13; Scott J. Ferrell/Congressional Quarterly/Newscom, 16; True Images/Alamy, 23;
Frederic Legrand/COMEO/Shutterstock Images, 25; iStockphoto, 26–27, 29, 45; Jason and
Bonnie Grower/Shutterstock Images, 31; Rashah McChesney/AP Images, 34–35; Africa Studio/
Shutterstock Images, 36; Thomas Deco/Shutterstock Images, 38

Editor: Maddie Spalding
Series Designer: Megan Ellis

Library of Congress Control Number: 2018966066

Publisher's Cataloging-in-Publication Data

Names: Hudak, Heather C., author.
Title: Cell phone privacy / by Heather C. Hudak
Description: Minneapolis, Minnesota: Abdo Publishing, 2020 | Series: Privacy in the digital age |
    Includes online resources and index.
Identifiers: ISBN 9781532118890 (lib. bdg.) | ISBN 9781532173073 (ebook) | ISBN
    9781644940808 (pbk.)
Subjects: LCSH: Wireless communication systems--Security measures--Juvenile literature.
    | Information policy--United States--Juvenile literature. | Privacy, Right of--United
    States--Juvenile literature. | Cellular telephone calls-- Juvenile literature. | Cell
    phones-- Juvenile literature.
Classification: DDC 005.8--dc23

CONTENTS

CHAPTER ONE

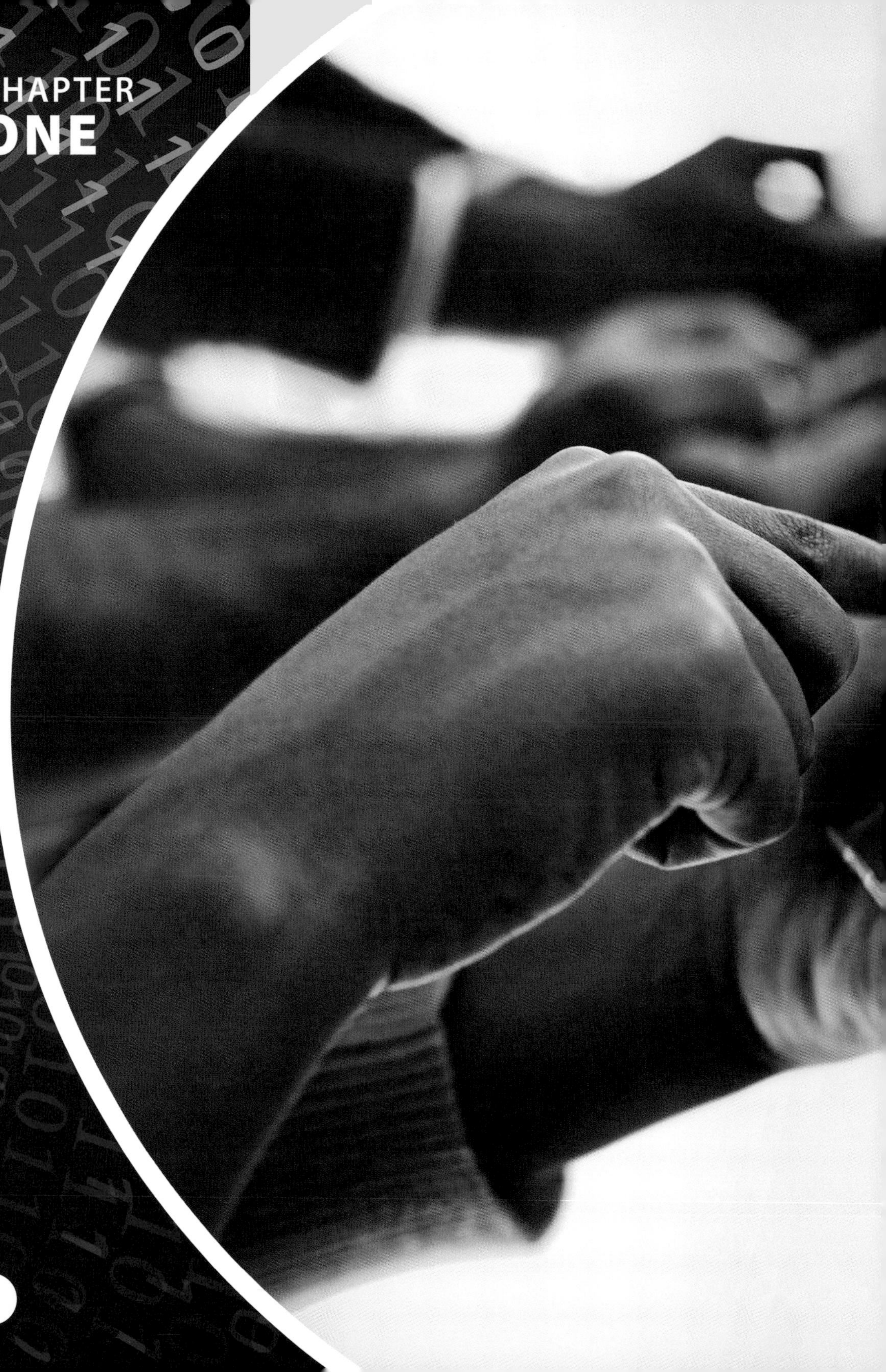

STOLEN IDENTITY

On January 8, 2018, Megan Clifford got a text from her cell phone carrier. It said that some of her account details had been changed. She needed to contact the carrier if she did not make the change herself. Clifford called her carrier right away. But it was too late. Hackers had moved her phone number to another phone. They had stolen her identity in just 30 minutes.

Clifford soon realized the hackers could get into her phone apps. Each app stored personal information. The hackers had access

Cell phones are common targets for hackers.

to her credit card numbers and birth date. They also had access to her photos. Clifford started to get emails from her bank. The hackers had used her personal information to withdraw money from her bank accounts. Clifford had to act fast. She had to change her passwords to shut out the hackers.

Clifford's life began to fall apart. She was no longer in control of her phone number. She had to contact every business she had accounts with to update her details. It took her more than one month to sort out. She had to pay thousands of dollars in fees.

WHAT IS CYBERCRIME?

Cybercrime is crime that happens on a computer or the internet. Many cybercrimes involve hacking. Hackers break into computer systems. Some damage computer systems or data. Others steal personal data, such as credit card numbers. This data is part of a person's identity. This type of crime is called identity theft. Another common cybercrime is cyberbullying. Cyberbullying occurs when people send or post hurtful messages about others online.

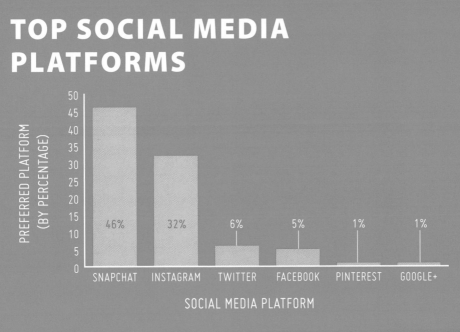

TOP SOCIAL MEDIA PLATFORMS

Chart — Preferred Platform (by percentage) vs Social Media Platform:
- SNAPCHAT: 46%
- INSTAGRAM: 32%
- TWITTER: 6%
- FACEBOOK: 5%
- PINTEREST: 1%
- GOOGLE+: 1%

The above graph shows the most popular social media platforms among US teens in 2018. Do you use these platforms? What personal information do you think they may collect?

WHAT HAPPENED?

Clifford was the victim of a cell phone porting scam. This is a common scam. It is used to gain access to someone's cell phone data. Hackers call the person's cell phone carrier. They pretend to be the owner of the phone. Carriers ask a few questions to make sure they are talking to the phone's owner. One question might be, "What is your pet's name?" Another could be, "What street did you grow up on?" Hackers can often find the answers on social media sites. Then they ask to have all calls and texts sent to their own phone. This gives them control of the number.

Many apps use cell phone numbers to confirm a person's identity. The app sends a text with a code to the cell phone. The person enters this code to gain access to an account. This is called multi-factor authentication. Hackers can have these codes sent to their own phones. They use the codes to reset account passwords. Then they have access to the accounts.

PRIVACY PROTECTION

Cell phones store personal data. Most actions people do on their phones produce data. Data is stored each time someone downloads an app. Shopping online or posting on social media also create data. This data is not always private. Phone carriers and other companies can access personal information. Scams can expose this information. But there are ways people can protect their cell phone data.

FURTHER EVIDENCE

Chapter One describes one way hackers can steal cell phone data. What was one of the main points of this chapter? What key evidence supports this point? Read the article at the website below. Does the information on the website support this point? Or does it present new evidence?

THE MOST COMMON MOBILE PHONE SCAMS
abdocorelibrary.com/cell-phone-privacy

CHAPTER
TWO

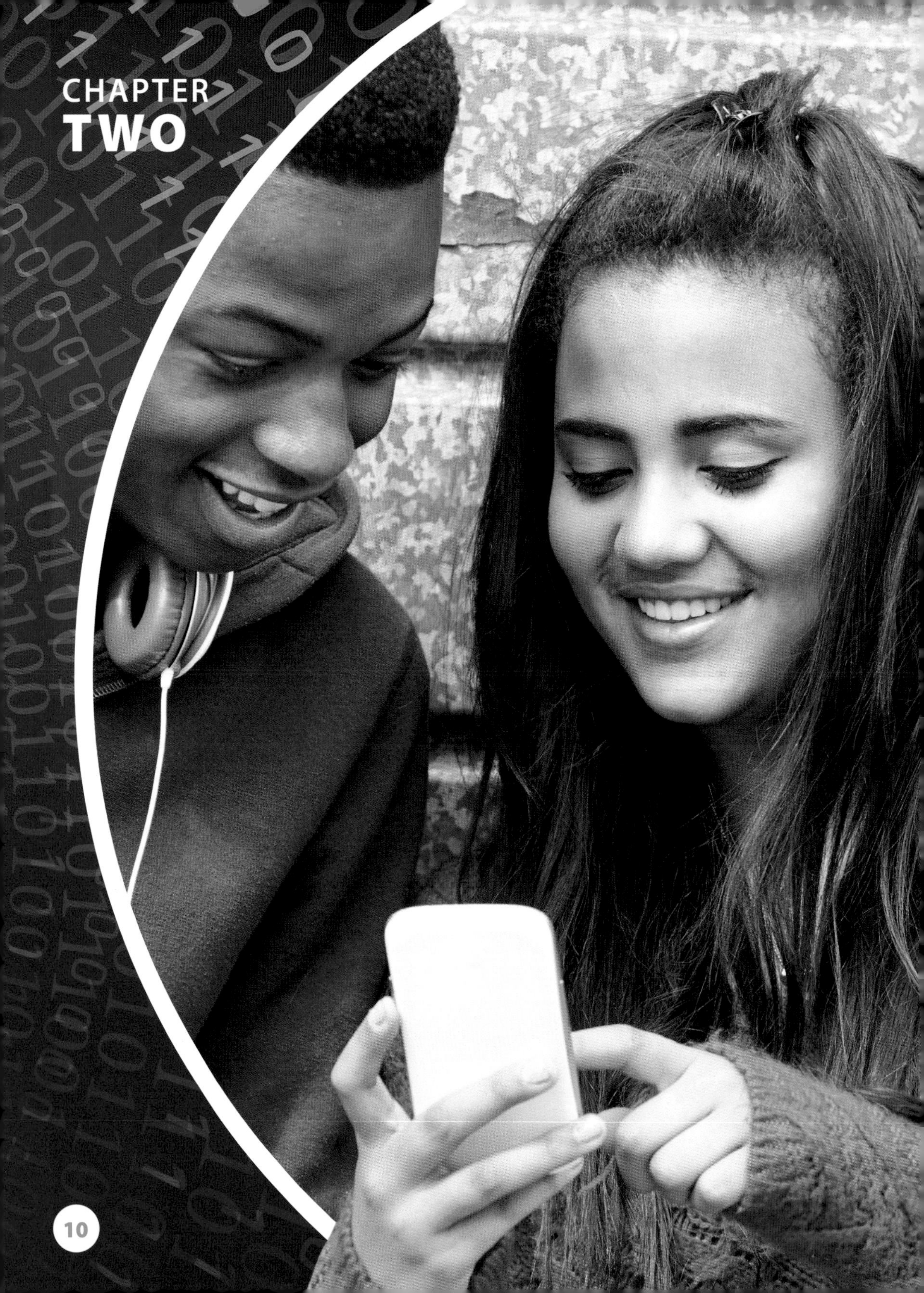

HANDHELD HISTORY

It may be hard to imagine a world without cell phones. More than 5 billion people around the world have a cell phone. That is two-thirds of the world's population. But cell phones as we know them today have only been around for a few decades.

Cell phones are wireless telephones. They convert calls and texts into electrical signals. The signals travel to the nearest cell tower. A cell tower is a pole with wires or cables. It carries electrical signals. The signals pass from one cell tower

Many people own cell phones and use them every day.

11

DAILY CELL PHONE USE

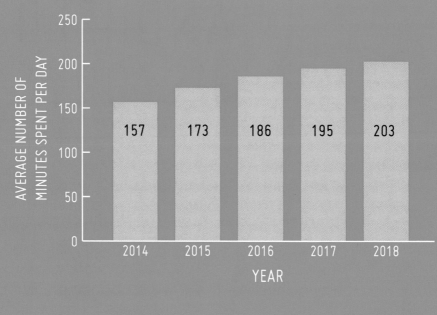

Many people use cell phones every day. The above graph shows the average amount of time US adults spend on cell phones each day and how this has changed through the years. Does this information surprise you? Why or why not?

to another until they reach their destination. This is most often a cell phone or tablet. The device converts the signal into a call or text. Cell phones are mobile. This means that people can easily move and carry them.

EARLY DEVICES

In 1973 the company Motorola made the first handheld cell phone. The phone was shaped like a brick.

Early cell phones had fewer features than smartphones.

It weighed more than 2 pounds (1 kg). It took ten hours to fully charge. It could be used for only 30 minutes.

Phone and computer companies worked to improve cell phone technology over the next few decades. Companies developed smaller cell phones with better batteries. By the early 2000s, cell phones had many functions. They could send and receive texts, take pictures, and play simple games. Soon the first smartphones began to appear. They had even more features. They had touch screens and ran all kinds of apps.

In 2007 the technology company Apple developed the first iPhone. People could do many tasks on this powerful smartphone. They could bank online, send emails, and shop. As a result, people began to store more data on their phones. Cell phone cybercrimes began to rise.

DATA THEFT

In 2016 a message appeared on some people's iPhone screens. It said that their device had been locked and they had to pay $50 to unlock it. But the phones were not actually locked. Cybercriminals had stolen users' personal data, including some of their passwords. They used this data to log into a user's iCloud account. iCloud is a data storage service. Then they activated the Find My iPhone app. This app helps people find their iPhone if they lose it. Criminals were able to create the threatening message. Phone users could simply type in their passcode. This unlocked their phone.

Criminals wanted to access private data and use it for personal gain.

STORAGE SPACE

Data such as photos and videos are stored on a phone's internal memory. This data is not stored anywhere else. If the phone stops working, the data is lost. For this reason, some people back up their phones to the cloud. Other phones have memory cards. Data is saved on these cards. Memory cards can be removed from phones.

PERSPECTIVES
LIVING IN THE CLOUD

The cloud is a phrase used to describe computers connected to the internet. These computers let users store data remotely. Users simply need an internet connection. People can access the cloud through a mobile app or a web browser. A web browser is a computer program used to access websites on the internet. Mark Hill is a technology expert. He explained why many companies rely on the cloud. He said, "An organization can store data and software in highly secure locations. . . . This is [a] . . . key factor that makes the cloud more desirable than the alternatives."

Members of the US Senate talked about mobile data protection at a hearing in 2011.

PRIVACY LAWS

As cell phones became more common, people grew concerned about their data's safety. They wondered how their data was being used. Privacy laws provided some protection. These laws control how companies and government agencies store and use private data.

They protect people from having their data misused or stolen. The California Online Privacy Protection Act (CalOPPA) was passed in 2004. It was the first act of its kind in the United States. It ensures that people or businesses that collect private data do not share it with anyone who should not have access to it. Websites that collect personal data are required to share their privacy policies with users. CalOPPA was extended to cover mobile apps in 2012. Mobile apps that collect personal data also need to share their privacy policies.

EXPLORE ONLINE

Chapter Two explores the history of cell phones. The article at the website below goes into more depth on this topic. How is the information from the website the same as the information in this chapter? What new information did you learn?

THE HISTORY AND EVOLUTION OF CELL PHONES
abdocorelibrary.com/cell-phone-privacy

CHAPTER
THREE

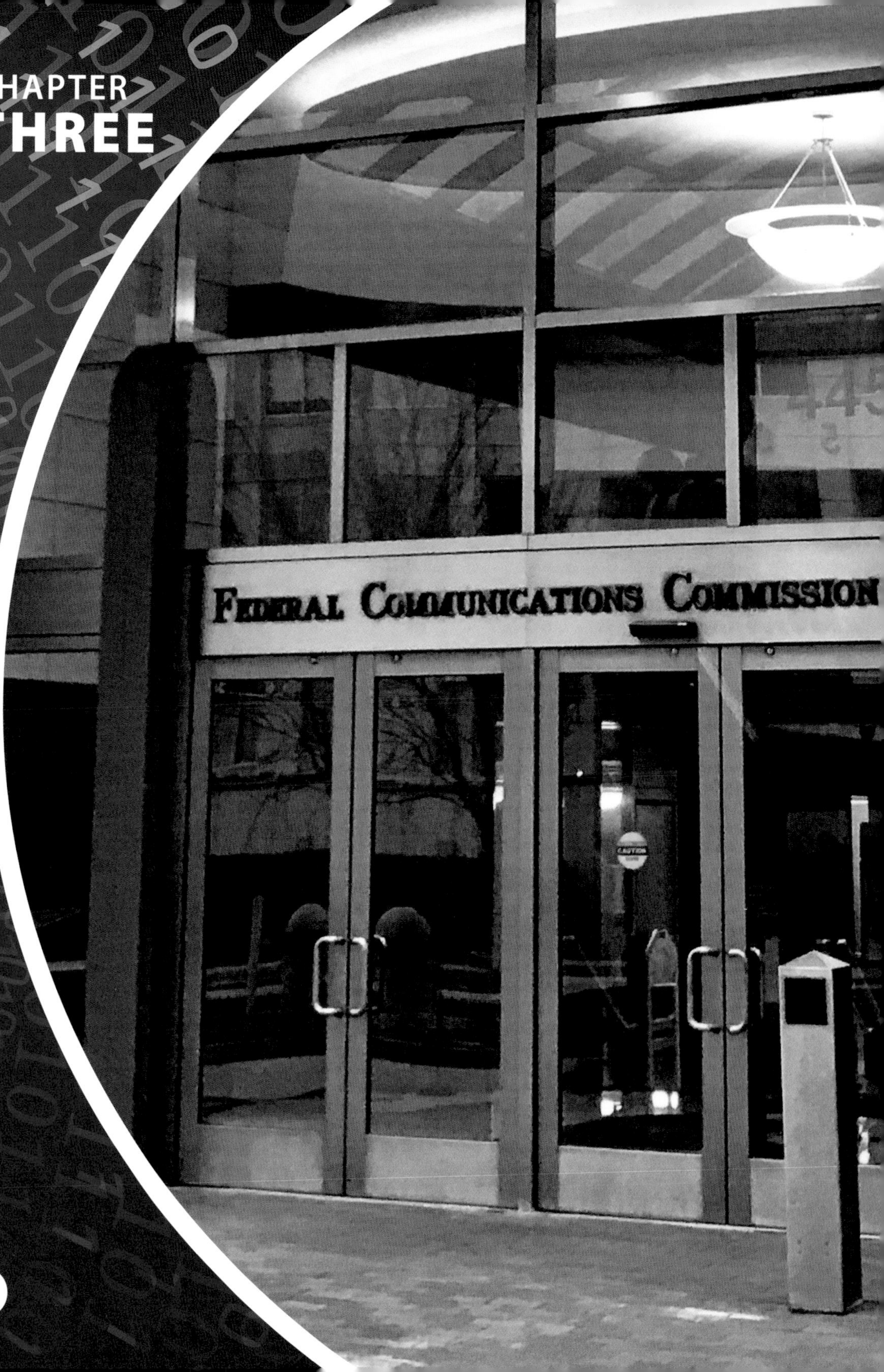

ACCESS TO INFORMATION

n 2002 the Federal Communications Commission (FCC) said US phone carriers had to begin using a special 911 phone system. It would give emergency services location data when people dial 911. This data would speed up responses to emergency calls.

Most people agreed that giving emergency services access to location data had benefits. People in an emergency may not know their location. Rescue crews could use their location data to find them. Police could use the data to stop crimes or track down suspects. But some privacy groups

The Federal Communications Commission headquarters is in Washington, DC.

raised concerns. The system allowed location data to be shared without a person's permission. People wondered about what other types of data might be shared. They worried about who would have access to that data. They demanded more information about how companies used their data.

CELL PHONE DATA

Location information is one type of data that is stored on cell phones. Other personal data on cell phones can include usernames and passwords. A person can log into accounts with this information. Photos, contact lists, and browsing history are other common types of cell phone data.

Cell phone data can reveal a lot about a person. It may show which political party a person supports. It may give information about the person's friends or family. This data can be used in many ways. For example, an app might sell a user's data to a political group that wants to sway the person's vote.

HACKERS

Hackers are always looking for new ways to steal cell phone data. Some may try to steal the phone itself. They can access data stored on a phone if they crack the phone's passcode. Other hackers use malware to steal data. Malware is software that infects computer systems. It can damage files and shut down systems. It can also be used to steal private data. Many hackers use phishing scams to upload malware onto devices. Some cell phone phishing scams involve texts. The hacker claims to be someone the person can trust. This tactic is called social engineering. For example, a phishing text may appear to be from a credit card company. It may say that the user's credit account has been hacked.

Some texts urge users to click on a link. Others tell users to text back. When users take these actions, malware is uploaded onto their device. People should always check links before clicking on them. Links that have spelling errors or look odd may be scams.

Some people attempt to scam others through phone calls. The caller may pretend to be someone the user trusts, such as a bank. The caller asks the person to provide private information. These types of scams are called voice

PERSPECTIVES
DIGIT SPOOFING

Caller identification (ID) shows incoming phone numbers. People may not answer the call if they do not recognize a number. But caller ID numbers can be altered. They may look similar to a number that is familiar to a victim. This tactic is called digit spoofing. People are more likely to answer calls from familiar-looking numbers. The caller may pretend to be someone the victim knows. Then the caller may ask for payment or private information. Adam Doupe is a cybersecurity expert. He says, "Phone scams are one of the big problems right now. They're much more effective than email scams."

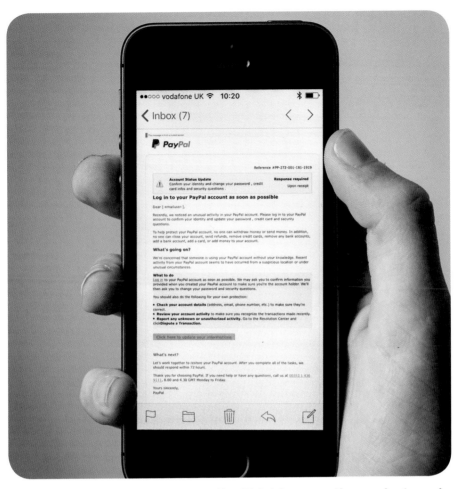

Some phishing scams are emails. Phishing emails are designed to trick many people.

phishing, or vishing. A caller pretending to be a bank may ask for a person's personal identification number (PIN). PINs give access to bank accounts. Banks do not ask people to give their PINs over the phone. People should never share PINs over the phone.

THE RIGHT TO PRIVACY

The Fourth Amendment protects a person's right to privacy. It says that the government and police cannot search or take private property without probable cause. Probable cause is the belief that a person has committed or is likely to commit a crime. This belief must be supported by facts. Then police can get a search warrant from a judge. This warrant gives police permission to search private property. Cell phones are private property.

In 1986 the US Congress passed the Electronic Communications Privacy Act (ECPA). The ECPA restricts the government's ability to read people's electronic communications, such as their emails. But the act does not clearly define electronic communications. This makes it hard to enforce.

In 2015 California Governor Jerry Brown signed an act into law. It is called the California Electronic Communications Privacy Act (CalECPA). CalECPA

California governor Jerry Brown has made data privacy one of his priorities while in office.

protects people's cell phone privacy. It says that state law enforcement agencies need a warrant to access people's cell phone data.

In 2018 the US Supreme Court ruled to limit the police's access to cell phone location data. The police can only access a person's phone without a warrant in an emergency. This ruling was a key step in the fight for better cell phone privacy.

CHAPTER
FOUR

PERMISSION GRANTED

Phone carriers know which cell tower is closest to a cell phone user. This information can help them track the user's location. Most carriers also gather details about people's calls and text messages. This includes a list of the phone numbers and the length of the calls. Carriers may collect information about the sites cell phone users visit and the apps they use. This type of information is called metadata.

Many carriers sell user metadata to other companies. These companies may include

Cell towers send data between cell phone carriers and users.

stores, marketers, and apps. Companies use cell phone data in many ways. Some might send texts to tell a person about a sale at a nearby store. Apps also collect data from users. Apps such as Uber use location data to find people who request their services.

Carriers are required to have privacy policies. Privacy policies explain how carriers use the data they collect. But these policies are not always clear. They also vary from one carrier to another. People cannot stop carriers from collecting data. But they may be able to control how carriers use the data. People can report

APP AGREEMENT

When people sign up to use apps, they agree to provide certain data. This data can include information such as their name or birth date. In this way, people give up some of their privacy rights. For example, a ride-share service may ask to access a user's location. An online store may need payment details. Other apps, such as Snapchat, track how people use the apps. This helps app developers improve the services they provide.

Apps collect a lot of data from cell phone users.

companies that violate privacy policies to the Federal Trade Commission (FTC). The FTC enforces privacy protection laws.

APPS AND MARKETING

Most apps collect data about the pages and advertisements a user views. The data is sent to the app's developer. The developer sells the data to marketers. Marketers advertise products for companies. Marketers use the data to make a profile of the user. They sell the profile to companies. This data helps companies create ads that the user may like. This strategy is called targeted advertising.

FEDERAL AGENCIES

Cell phone data is not only useful to app developers and marketers. Federal agencies may also use cell phone data. The Federal Bureau of Investigation (FBI) and the National Security Agency (NSA) are federal agencies. They investigate security threats. They may need cell phone data to help stop an act of terrorism. They need a warrant to access this data.

In 2001 President George W. Bush started the President's Surveillance Program (PSP). The PSP was a response to terrorist attacks on September 11, 2001. Terrorists hijacked airplanes. They crashed planes into buildings in New York City and Arlington, Virginia. Another plane crashed into a field in Pennsylvania. The attacks killed nearly 3,000 people. The PSP gave the NSA the right to monitor the communications of people who might have ties to terrorist groups.

George W. Bush, who started the PSP, was the US president from 2001 to 2009.

The NSA monitored millions of Americans who were not criminal suspects. The NSA collected data from cell phone carriers. This data included cell phone users' names, addresses, and call records.

In 2013 Edward Snowden leaked details about the NSA's surveillance program. Snowden was working for the NSA. He said the NSA was forcing cell phone carriers to share cell phone data. Many people were surprised to learn how the government was monitoring them. They believed the NSA's surveillance violated their right to privacy.

BORDER PATROL SEARCHES

In 2017 CBP agents searched more than 30,000 phones and other devices. This was about a 60 percent increase from 2016. Activists say that these searches are an invasion of people's privacy. They think CBP should be required to have warrants to do these searches. Many people also think CBP needs more government oversight. David Long is a spokesperson for CBP. He said, "Agents have broad law enforcement authorities. . . . They have the authority to question individuals, make arrests, and take and consider evidence."

United States Customs and Border Protection (CBP) is another federal agency. CBP agents patrol US borders. They try to reduce illegal immigration. They are also in charge of security. They make sure people entering the country are not threats. Agents can search people's property. They do not need a warrant to search a person's cell phone. But they need to have reason to believe that the person has committed a crime.

STRAIGHT TO THE
SOURCE

In 2013 Edward Snowden gave an interview with the newspaper the *Guardian*. He explained why he leaked information about the NSA's surveillance program:

> *The NSA has built an infrastructure that allows it to intercept almost everything. With this capability, the vast majority of human communications are automatically ingested without targeting. . . . I can get your emails, passwords, phone records, credit cards. I don't want to live in a society that does these sort of things. . . . I do not want to live in a world where everything I do and say is recorded. That is not something I am willing to support or live under.*

> Source: Edward Snowden. "Edward Snowden, NSA Files Source: 'If They Want to Get You, in Time They Will.'" *The Guardian*. The Guardian, June 10, 2013. Web. Accessed November 1, 2018.

Point of View

Snowden thinks that the NSA collects too much data from Americans. Read back through this chapter. Do you agree? Why or why not?

SECURITY MEASURES

Some activist groups fight for cell phone privacy rights. These groups include the Electronic Frontier Foundation (EFF), the Electronic Privacy Information Center, and the American Civil Liberties Union (ACLU). They advocate for new data privacy laws.

In 2016 the General Data Protection Regulation (GDPR) was passed. The GDPR is a data privacy law. It applies to companies in Europe. It also applies to companies that collect data about European residents. It says that companies have to tell users about the

The American Civil Liberties Union helps protect people's data privacy.

People should use a different password for each account.

data they collect. Companies that do not follow this rule have to pay fines.

PROTECTING PRIVACY

People can take steps to keep their cell phone data private. They should never leave their cell phone unattended. They should keep their phone in a safe place. It is also important to be aware of common phone scams. Then people will be able to recognize and ignore scams.

Strong passwords can help protect cell phone data. A password keeps a phone locked until the user is ready to use it. This can prevent people from stealing data if the phone is lost or stolen. Each account should be protected by a strong password. People should not save their passwords in their phones. If a phone falls into the wrong hands, stored passwords can make it easy for accounts to be hacked.

Some hackers create apps to break into people's phones. People should only download apps from trusted sources.

Google Maps is an app that collects users' location data.

They should read an app's privacy policy. People may be able to limit how their data is used and who can access it. But that does not always stop the app from collecting data.

Cell phones have privacy settings. Users can turn off location sharing in these settings. But in 2018, cell phone users made a discovery. They found that some apps store location data even when location sharing is turned off. For example, the Google Maps app collects location data. It uses this data to provide directions. It stores the data in its history. Google Maps users can turn off their location history at any time. But the app will still store some data. Google uses this data to improve its services. Some users argue that this violates their right to privacy.

CELL PHONE SECURITY

Many cell phones have security features. Security features protect cell phone data. Fingerprint recognition is one type of security feature. Sensors map and recognize users' fingerprints. Each person has different fingerprint patterns. To unlock a phone, the user places a finger on a sensor. The sensor compares the

TESTING SECURITY FEATURES

Some researchers look for weaknesses in security features. This can help companies improve these features. In 2017 some researchers studied fingerprint recognition sensors. These sensors are small. They only capture part of a person's fingerprint. Fingerprints share some common features. The researchers created a digital fingerprint. They tried scanning this fake fingerprint. They fooled scanners about 65 percent of the time.

fingerprint pattern to the ones stored in the phone. The phone only unlocks if the pattern is a match.

Some cell phones have a facial recognition feature. Users take pictures of their face using the phone's camera. The phone stores these images. Users look at a sensor to unlock the phone. The sensor compares the user's features to the stored images. Each person has unique facial features. The phone only unlocks if the images match. A similar feature is iris recognition. The iris is a part of a person's eye. A phone unlocks when it recognizes a user's iris.

High-tech features provide an extra layer of security. Stronger data privacy laws may also help protect cell phone users' data in the future. Data collection has benefits. Companies can use cell phone data to provide better services. But many people see this data collection as an invasion of privacy. The debate about cell phone privacy is ongoing.

STRAIGHT TO THE
SOURCE

Steve Jobs was the cofounder of the technology company Apple. He had strong opinions about privacy. He discussed his views at a conference in 2010:

Privacy means people know what they're signing up for, in plain English, and repeatedly. I'm an optimist; I believe people are smart, and some people want to share more data than other people do. Ask them. Ask them every time. Make them tell you to stop asking them if they get tired of your asking them. Let them know precisely what you're going to do with their data.

Source: Mike Murphy. "Steve Jobs Tried to Warn Mark Zuckerberg about Privacy in 2010." *Quartz*. Quartz, March 23, 2018. Web. Accessed November 2, 2018.

Consider Your Audience

Adapt this passage for a different audience, such as your friends. Write a blog post conveying this same information for the new audience. How does your post differ from the original text and why?

FAST FACTS

- More than 5 billion people, or two-thirds of the world's population, have cell phones.

- Cell phone carriers collect certain types of data. This includes data about calls and text messages.

- Cell phone carriers have privacy policies that explain how they use customers' data. Carriers also must disclose the data they collect. They may sell this data to other companies.

- When people download apps on their phones, they give the apps permission to collect certain data. This data is sent to the app's developer. The developer may sell the data to marketers.

- Some hackers steal cell phone data and use it for personal gain. They may use special software or other tools to gain access to data.

- Police and the government sometimes collect cell phone data. In most cases, warrants are needed to search people's cell phones.

- Security measures such as passwords and sensors can help protect cell phone data.

- Today, many groups advocate for better data privacy laws.

STOP AND
THINK

Dig Deeper

After reading this book, what questions do you still have about cell phone privacy? With an adult's help, find a few reliable sources that can help you answer your questions. Write a paragraph about what you learned.

Take a Stand

This book talks about how US Customs and Border Protection agents do not need warrants to search people's cell phones. Do you think warrants should always be required to access cell phone data? Why or why not?

You Are There

Chapter One describes how a hacker can use cell phone data to steal a person's identity. Imagine that a friend's cell phone data was stolen. What advice would you give your friend? What security measures could your friend take to prevent this theft in the future?

Why Do I Care?

Chapter Two describes how the invention of smartphones changed the way people live. How do smartphones affect your life? How would your life be different without this invention?

GLOSSARY

app
a software program on a mobile device that has a specific purpose or function

data
information that can be stored and studied

hacker
someone who breaks into computer systems

identity
the features that define who a person is

infrastructure
the structures and systems needed to run a system

malware
software that damages or destroys computer systems

metadata
information about data, such as the author of the data or when it was created

phishing
a type of fraud that happens when someone poses as a trusted source via email, text, or phone in order to access private data

surveillance
the act of carefully watching someone or something

warrant
a legal document that allows law enforcement to make an arrest or search private property

ONLINE RESOURCES

To learn more about cell phone privacy, visit our free resource websites below.

Visit **abdocorelibrary.com** or scan this QR code for free Common Core resources for teachers and students, including vetted activities, multimedia, and booklinks, for deeper subject comprehension.

Visit **abdobooklinks.com** or scan this QR code for free additional online weblinks for further learning. These links are routinely monitored and updated to provide the most current information available.

LEARN MORE

Rodger, Ellen. *Top Secret Science in Cybercrime and Espionage*. New York: Crabtree Publishing, 2019.

Smibert, Angie. *Inside Computers*. Minneapolis, MN: Abdo Publishing, 2019.

INDEX

About the Author

Heather C. Hudak has written hundreds of books for schools and libraries. When she is not writing, you can find her camping in the mountains with her husband and rescue pets or traveling the world. She loves eating pasta in Italy, visiting ancient temples in Indonesia, and searching for animals on the African savannah.